A PICTURE BOOK
OF DOLLS AND
DOLLS' HOUSES

British Library Cataloguing-in-Publication Data
A catalogue record for this book is available from the
British Library

Dolls

A doll is a model of a human being, often used as a toy for children. Dolls have traditionally been used in magic and religious rituals throughout the world, and dolls made of materials like clay and wood have been found in the Americas, Asia, Africa and Europe. The earliest documented dolls go back to the ancient civilizations of Egypt, Greece and Rome. Such dolls – specifically used as toys for girls, with moveable limbs and clothing, were notably documented in ancient Greece, created both as rudimentary playthings, but also as elaborate art. Today's doll manufacturing has its roots in Germany though, dating back to the fifteenth century. With industrialisation and the appearance of new materials like porcelain and plastic, dolls were increasingly mass-produced, and from this point onwards, right until the present day, dolls have become increasingly popular as simple toys and expensive collectibles.

The earliest dolls were made from available materials like clay, stone, wood, bone, ivory, leather and wax. Archaeological evidence places dolls as the foremost candidate for the world's oldest toy! Wooden paddle dolls (a type of female figurine found in burials) have been discovered in Egyptian tombs which date to as early as 2000 BCE. Dolls with movable appendages and removable outfits date back to at least 200 BCE. Greek dolls were made of clay and articulated at the hips and shoulders, and there are clear stories, dating from around

100 AD that describe such dolls being used by little girls as playthings. The modern dolls predecessors, the German models, have been documented as far back as the thirteenth century, with wooden dolls dating from the fifteenth century. From this point onwards, increasingly elaborate dolls were made for Nativity scenes, especially in Italy, and dolls with detailed, fashionable clothes were sold in France from the sixteenth century.

The German and Dutch 'peg wooden dolls' (using a jointing technique where the arms and/or legs are attached to the body with pegs), were cheap and simply made and were popular toys for poorer children in Europe. Wood continued to be the dominant material for doll construction until the nineteenth century, when it became increasingly combined with other materials such as leather, wax and porcelain. This allowed for doll construction to be far more intricate. It is unknown when dolls' glass eyes first appeared, but brown was the dominant eye colour for dolls up until the Victorian era when blue eyes became more popular, inspired by Queen Victoria. Interestingly, up until the middle of the nineteenth century, European dolls were predominantly made to represent grown-ups. Childlike dolls and the later ubiquitous baby doll did not appear until the 1850s, but by the late century, childlike dolls had overtaken the market.

The earliest celebrity dolls were 'Paper dolls'; dolls usually made of cardboard like materials, with separate clothes usually held onto the dolls by folding tabs. The nineteenth century ballerina paper dolls were among the earliest celebrity dolls, and the 1930s Shirley Temple doll sold in the millions, becoming one of the most successful celebrity dolls. A similar genre of doll, 'fashion dolls', were primarily designed to be dressed, and reflect fashion trends – usually modelled after teenage girls or adult women. Contemporary fashion dolls are typically made of vinyl, the most famous example of which, is the 'Barbie doll'. Barbies were made from 1959 onwards, by the American toy company Mattel, and have dominated the market from their inception. The only doll to challenge Barbie's dominance was the 'Bratz' make, reaching forty percent of the market share in 2006.

Despite their construction for children, some dolls, such as the nineteenth century bisque dolls, made by French manufacturers such as Bru and Jumeau, may be worth over £22,000 today. Dolls have also made it into the political and artistic spheres, with artists such as Hans Bellmer, who made surrealistic dolls with interchangeable limbs in the 1930s and 1940s, in opposition to the Nazi party's idolisation of the perfect Aryan body. East Village artist Greer Lankton became famous in the 1980s for her theatrical window displays of drug addicted, anorexic and mutant dolls, reflecting the deteriorating social conditions of America's 'cultural capital.' Many books (mostly aimed at children) have also dealt with dolls, for example tales such as *Whilhelmina. The Adventures of a Dutch Doll,* by Nora Pitt-Taylor and the *Raggedy Ann* books by Johnny

Gruelle, first published in 1918. Our fascination with dolls is showing no signs of waning in the present day, and it is hoped that the reader enjoys this book.

Dollhouses

A dollhouse or doll's house is often a toy home, made in miniature. For the last century, dollhouses have primarily been the domain of children but their collection and crafting is also a hobby for many adults. Dollhouses can range from the amateur miniaturist placing a few decorated boxes on top of one another to be enjoyed by one person, up to incomparable multi-million dollar structures viewed by millions of people each year. Today's children's dollhouses originally originated from the *baby house* display cases of sixteenth century Europe, designed to show idealised interiors. Smaller dollhouses with more realistic exteriors appeared in Europe in the eighteenth century. Early dollhouses were all handmade, but following the Industrial Revolution and the Second World War, they were increasingly mass-produced and became more standardized and affordable.

Miniature homes, furnished with domestic articles and resident inhabitants, both people and animals, have been made for thousands of years. The earliest known examples were found in the Egyptian tombs of the Old Kingdom, created nearly five thousand years ago. These wooden representations found in the Pyramids, including models of servants, furnishings, boats, livestock and pets were almost certainly were made for religious purposes. But the earliest known European dollhouses appeared in the sixteenth century. They were each handmade and unique, and consisted of cabinet display cases made up of individual rooms. A prime example of the genre is Duke Albrecht V of Bavaria's realistic, yet miniature copy of his royal residence in 1557. Most other dollhouses of this period showed idealised interiors complete with extremely detailed furnishings and accessories. It should be pointed out that such items were solely intended as the play things of adults; they were an expression of status and wealth, very far from a children's toy. Fully furnished, such models were worth the price of a modest-full-size house's construction.

Smaller doll houses such as the 'Tate house', with more realistic exteriors, appeared in Europe in the eighteenth century. Germany was the producer of the most prized dollhouses and doll house miniatures up until the First World War, and notable German companies included Märklin, Rock and Graner, and others. Their products were not only avidly collected in Central Europe, but regularly exported to Britain and North America. After the War, Germany's dire financial and industrial situation impeded both production and export, and she ceased to be the main producer of dollhouses. Post-World War Two, dollhouses began to be mass-produced on a much larger scale than previously, with notably less detailed craftsmanship. By the 1950s, a typical commercial dollhouse was made of painted sheet metal filled with plastic furniture. Such houses were inexpensive enough that the great majority of girls from developed countries (those not struggling with rebuilding after the war) could own one.

Today, there are dozens of miniature trade shows held each year by various miniature organisations and enthusiasts. Here, artisans and dealers display and sell miniatures to others in the trade, as well as the public. Often, how-to seminars and workshops, for those keen to 'build their own' are part of the show features. There are also numerous internet forums, blogs and other online-social medias concentrated solely on dollhouses and miniatures. Some miniatures are true treasures worth hundreds of thousands of dollars, with a rare few dating back thousands of years. Current children's dollhouses are commonly 1:18 scale, whereas the most common standard for adult collectors is 1:12 scale.

There are three major museum quality palatial dollhouses in the world, where this art form has been taken to the highest calibre: Queen Mary's Dolls' House; the Dollhouse of Colleen Moore; and Astolat Dollhouse Castle. Each can weigh up to 2,000 pounds, appraise at well over a million pounds, and contain furnishings that are as true-to-life as humanly possible. However, as an interesting note, one of the things that you will never see in the interiors of these world-class dollhouses, is a doll. The inability to precisely replicate the human body and face in miniature would detract from the accuracy of these perfect miniature settings. Queen Mary's Dolls' House is part of the Royal Collection Trust and is on show at Windsor Castle, England. When first put on display it was visited by 1.6 million people in seven months. Moore's dollhouse is called the 'Fairy Castle' and would cost over £7 million if built today. It is visited by an estimated 1.5 million people each year where it resides in Chicago at the Museum of Industry and Science. The Astolat Dollhouse Castle is on display at the Nassau County Museum of Art on Long Island, New York. All were built to 1:12 scale, although they vary in overall size. The Queen Mary's Dolls' House is approximately 5' tall, contains 16 rooms, and required 4 years to construct. The Colleen Moore dollhouse is 7' tall, has twelve rooms, and took 7 years to construct. The Astolat Castle Dollhouse is 9' tall, has 29 rooms, and required more than 10 years to build. We hope the reader enjoys this book on dollhouses, and is inspired to create their own (perhaps more modest!) miniature dwelling.

1. ENGLISH. Early 18th century. T.260—1923. *Given by Mrs. Greg.*

2. ENGLISH. About 1770-80. T.54—1917. *Given by Miss Ethel Dixon.*

3. ENGLISH. About 1830. T.235—1918. *Given by Miss M. A. Rooth in memory of her mother, Mrs. Goodwin Rooth of Hampstead.*

4A. ENGLISH. Period of George IV. (1820-30). T.215—1915. *Given by the Family of the late Major and Mrs. W. Mackay Mackenzie.*
4B. ENGLISH. About 1860-70. T.249—1922. *Given by Miss Gwendolen Barraclough.*

5. ENGLISH. (Dressed as a pedlar woman.) 19th century.
T.6—1910. *Given by Mrs. Allden.*

6. ENGLISH. About 1875. T.148—1925. *Given by Mrs. Galloway.*

7. DUTCH (Province of Zeeland). 19th century. T.255 & 256—1923. *Given by Miss Eliza F. J. Frere.*

8. SWISS. (Dressed as a Bernese married woman.) 19th century.
Given by Miss M. Narcombe. T.2—1913.

9. TOKIO. (Japanese Court Dress.) 19th century. 1310—1904.

10. NUREMBERG. Dated 1673. W. 41 in. 1933.

11. KITCHEN IN DOLL'S HOUSE (Plate 10). W.41—1922.

12. DOLL'S ROOM, ENGLISH. Period of Queen Anne (1702–1714). W.42—1922.

13. MARIONETTE THEATRE (Set for an Interior Scene). Venetian. First half of the 18th century. W.31—1924.

14. MARIONETTE THEATRE (Set for the Piazza San Marco, Venice, with figures from the Commedia Dell'arte). Venetian. First half of the 18th century. w.31—1924.

15. THE POWELL COLLECTION OF DOLLS.   English.   1750–1850.   w.183—1919.   *Given by Harry James Powell, Esq.*

16. ENGLISH. Late 18th century. w.49—1925. *Given by Mme. Georges Patry.*

17. INTERIOR OF PLATE 16. W.49—1925.

18. DINING ROOM OF PLATE 16. W.49—1925.

19. DOLL'S ROOM. English. 19th century. W.34—1917. *Given by H.M. Queen Mary.*

99843584R00019

Made in the USA
Columbia, SC
12 July 2018